Small Animals that Hide

Elsie Nelley

Contents

Small Animals

Some small animals hide from big animals.

The small animals hide
to stay safe.

Color

Lots of green bugs sit on green leaves.

Birds cannot see the bugs on the leaves.

A fox is a small animal.

It has a brown coat.

In winter

the fox has a new coat.

The new coat is white
like the snow.

Big animals cannot see
the white fox in the snow.

Shape

A stick insect
is a small animal.

It looks like a brown stick.

The stick insect can hide
on the branch of a tree.

A snail is a small animal.

It has a **shell** on its back.

The snail hides inside its shell.

Now the snail is safe

from birds.

Crabs hide
from big, hungry birds.

Crabs can dig very fast.
They dig down
into the wet sand.

Size

A baby kangaroo is small.

A mother kangaroo
has a **pouch**.
The baby kangaroo can get
into its mother's pouch
to hide from dogs.

Lots of small animals
are good at hiding.

Glossary

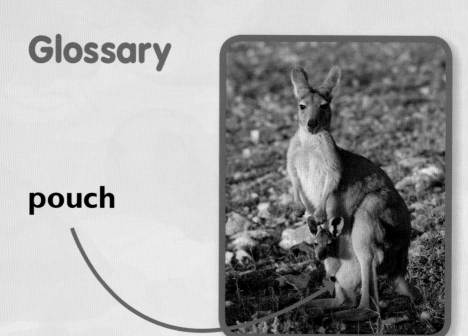

pouch

shell